# Menace of Maoist Insurgency in India

# Menace of Maoist Insurgency in India

Brig. R.A. Singh VSM (Retd.)

Raj Publications
New Delhi - 110002 (INDIA)

**Menace of Maoist Insurgency in India**



First Published in 2021

ISBN 978-93-82281-59-7

**₹ 225**



*Published by* : **Raj Publications**
108, 4855/24, Ansari Road,
Daryaganj, New Delhi - 110002
Tel. : 011-23250939, 9811010939
E-Mail: rajpublications@gmail.com

*Laser Typesetting* : Aarati Computers, Delhi-110 009

*Printed at* : Balaji Offset, Delhi

# Contents

# Preface

From the earlier historical days guerrilla warfare has been an important feature of war fought by every class of man against the oppressors. Infact it produces quick, dramatic results at low cost. It gave communism its major ally, mainland China. It sneaked into North Vietnam, Cuba and most of Laos. More extensive and prolonged guerrilla war was waged in the Far East since the nineteen twenties by the Chinese Communist, in whose leadership Mao Tse Tung played an increasingly dominant part. It developed in 1927 when Chiang-Kai Shek on defeating the Northern War lords in tidal advance from Canton, sought to suppress the communist elements in his National Revolution Army. It was turned against the Japanese from 1937 onwards, when Nationalist and Communist forces again made common cause in an uneasy alliance against the foreign invaders. The Communists operating in guerrilla way, did much to relieve Japanese pressure on Chiang Kai-Shek regular forces by harrassing the invading army. During the struggle the communists also played their hand with a view to the future, spreading their influence among the people in the occupied areas so effectively that when Japan eventually collapsed under American air and sea attacks, they were better placed to profit from the result and fill the vaccum, than Chiang Kai-Shek Nationalist Army.

In today's context, it is likely that insurgency may flare up in number of countries in near future, which may get moral and material support from the communists from at least outside. This may happen in countries where government consistently fails in its obligation to ensure at least minimally decent standard of life for its people, particularly in remote areas. If there exist even the nucleus of revolutionary party which is able to supply doctrine and organisation, only one ingrediant is needed, the instrument for violent revolutionary action.

Insurgency is also governed by general laws of warfare but since it starts with poverty stricken and aggrieved people, it may frame its own rules of the game in the beginning. He takes up arms in response to wide spread popular protest and discontentment against an oppressor, impetuously hurling himself with all his might against that symbolizes the established order  what in their strategy- it must be based primarily on alertness, mobility and quick action. It must be adjusted to operational situation, the terrain, the existing line of communications relative strength the weather and the situation of the people.

Tactics have to be modified to each individual situation in counter insurgency operations. There is no sanctity or permanance to the form of tactics. It depends on the technique peculiar to the area and the tactics of insurgents and their weapon system. It is often tempting to study past incidents/battles and dwell on these. It is only important to apply past wisdom to the changing pattern that the future unfolds. Sun Tzu wrote,

> "The supreme art of war is to subdue the enemy without fighting. Indiscriminate use of force that does not identify targets will always alienate people and such therefore accounted as a debit in long-term balance sheet. Quantum of force must be considered in its relationships to people and not to the area of ground of operation."

Today an understanding of art of insurgency or guerrilla warfare is vital to a soldier, essential to the statesman, necessary for many government officials and useful to many educated men. The troops involved in counter insurgency operations require intense physical and theoritical training. Course of instruction be developed in possible zones of operations to get maximum degree of geo-climatical orientation as well as tactical survival for the type of terrain obtaining in counter insurgency operations. The training should also be followed by psychological instructions to give the soldiers firm conviction on the reasons for operations. They need to understand its place in a free and democratic society and fundamental values they are defending. Methods like use of new technology, enhanced mobility, proper use of air power/support, use of psychological warfare, importance of knowing local languages, detailed knowledge of the area, proper use of intelligence and proper use of civil authorities. Most indians are volatile by temperament, some what depressed by failure and perheps over confident in success. This espect should also be well understood and explained with due caution to our men.

Although the subject of the book pertains to guerrilla warfare/insurgency and certain military terminology has been used, but attempt has been made to potray the events in the language that be readily understood by all. Certain assistance of various books, magazines, articles and newspapers has been taken over a period of time. Identity of the source were inadvertently missed out. Not with standing,

I am indebited to them for the indirect contribution.

I am an exserviceman who served in the Indian army for nearly 36 years, that too in the Infantry. Seeing the events taking turn from bad to worse in our insurgency prone states, I could not resist sharing my own long experience in counter insurgency operations, and decided to put it in writing so that it may be of some use and interest to someone. I have abstained from passing any opinion or judgement on various events which in recent past have not unfoled well in own counter insurgency operations in Chattisgarh and Jharkhand, unless it were absolutily inescapabel to complete the text and the narrative. The data has also been checked and compared with the existing records for its correctness. Any human error is requested to be overlooked.

I shall be failing if, I do not mention about my wife 'Rama' who has always been a source of inspiration for me and has indirectly contributed a lot in production of this book. I owe my gratitudes to her.

----- **Brig. R. A. Singh**
**VSM (Retd.)**

# Abbreviations

| | | |
|---|---|---|
| CIOps | : | Counter Insurgency Operations |
| IB | : | International Border |
| LOC | : | Line of Control |
| LAC | : | Line of Actual Control |
| SF | : | Security Forces |
| NE | : | North East |
| J&K | : | Jammu & Kashmir |
| PWG | : | peoples War Group |
| MCC | : | Maoist Communist Centre |
| CPI | : | Communist Party of India |
| PGLA | : | Peoples Liberation Guerrilla Army |
| HB | : | Heliborne |
| Heptr | : | Helicoper |
| IAF | : | Indian Air Force |

| | | |
|---|---|---|
| Armed | : | Armed |
| Recee | : | Reconnaissance |
| Trn | : | Terrain |
| RPF | : | Railways Protection Force |
| CRPF | : | Central Reserve Police Force |
| PLA | : | Peoples Liberation Army |
| Govt. | : | Government |
| SE Asia | : | South East Asia |
| Nuc | : | Nuclear |
| Emp | : | Employ |
| Dply | : | Deployment |
| Eqpt | : | Equipment |
| Strat | : | Strategy |
| Def | : | Defence |
| Iden | : | Identification |

# 1

# Insurgency- An Art of War

Guerrilla Warfare has been as old as all other types of wars. In second world war guerrilla warfare became so wide spread as to be an almost universal feature. It developed in all the European countries that were occupied by the Germans and most of the far Eastern countries that were occupied by the Japanese. Mean while however a more extensive and prolonged guerrilla war had been waged in the far east since the nineteen twenties by the chinese communists, in whose leadership Mao-Tse Tung played an inreasingly dominant part.

The guerrilla warfare in South East Asia, since 1945 have been quite different from the past wars and Mao Tse Tung, the communist leader has been largely responsible for the changes. It is fundamentaly different now and has been called as Revolutionary War, subverssive war or simply modern war. The new type of warfare consists largely the impact which agents of communist subversions can develop at all levels of human activity, political, economic, intellectual psychological and military with an idea in mind of overthrowing present government and replacing them by others which they consider to have correct political orientation from communists point of view.

Guerrilla Warfare must always be dynamic and will maintain momentum. Static intervals are more deterimental to its success than in case of regular warfare, as they allow the opponent to tighten his grip on the country and give rest to the troops, while seeking help of populace not to help the guerrillas. Strategically, guerrilla operation reverses the normal practice of warfare by seeking to avoid battle and other pitched encounter with the counter insurgency force where it is likely to suffer loses. The predominant tactics employed by the guerrilla is laying an ambush, where they can hit and run. The principle of concenrtration also does not hold good in guerrilla warfare, since dispersal in an essential condition of survival and success for guerrillas.

In coventional tactics disperssion of forces invite destruction, wheras it is desirable in guerilla tactics to confuse the CI force and to preserve the illusion that guerrilla are ubiquitos. Mao says "withdraw when enemy advances harrass him when he stops, strike him when he is weary, persue him when he withdraws." Rugged and forest areas are best suited for insurgents security which affords them opportunity for a surprise and suitable hides. Guerrilla war is a kind of war waged by the few but dependent on the support of masses.

The prospects and progress of guerrilla movement depends on the attitutde of the people in the area where insurgency breeds and their willingness to help gurerrillas by providing them intelligence and supplies and at the same time denying information to security forces about guerrillas hides and base camps. Generally the guerrilla warfare has been a weapon of the weaker side, and as such it depends on hide and seek and hit and run tactics. A potential insurgency situation exists in any country where the govt consistently fails in its obligations to ensure at least a minimally decent standard of life for its own citizens.

Guerrilla Warfare can be conducted in any terrain, in any climate, in any weather. Its basic element is man and a man is endowed with intelligence, emotions and will. Guerrilla leaders spend a great deal of time in organisation instructions, agitations and propganda work then they do fighting, since their most important job is to win over the people. Mao-Tse Tung has aptly compared guerrillas to fish and people to the water in which they swim. If the political temperature is right, the fish however few in number, will thrive and proliferate. It is therefor the principal concern of all guerrilla leaders to get the water to the right temperature and to keep it as such. These leaders are unyielding in their policies- resolute, loyal, sincere and robust. These are generally well educated in revolutionary technique, self confident, able to establish severe descipline and able to cope with counter propaganda. In short these leaders must be models for the people.

The political goal must be clearly and precisely indicated and professed by the guerrilla to masses or else it will fail. If it does not co incide with the aspirations of the people, their sympathy, cooperation and assistance can not be gained which is very important for the guerrillas to exist and flourish.

As regards the equipment of the insurgents/guerillas they are lightly armed with personal weapon and other tools and items as per the assigned tasks. The supply of weapons and ammunition is most difficult, since for their other administration support of food, water and medical, they can get from the sympathisers population of the area. The insurgents also carry destruction material for railway tracks, bridges etc for the assigned task whenever needed.

The propganda materials are also very important. At a higher level they have own printing places and for other advertisement they carry own paint and brushes.

Preparation for nuclear and conventional warfare are becoming very costly affair and reciprocal devastation has deferred any ventures. Therefore both forms of warfare are becoming increasingly less practical instruments of national policy. To check and curtail conventional war many treaties are in force by various nations, though not very effective on ground. By contrast guerrilla warfare has produced quick, dramatic results at low cost. Guerrilla warfare incites no nuclear retaliatron. Though communist guerrilla warfare is new weapon and not to be confused with old guerrilla concepts. It is a delibrate military effort inspired by international communism, using local adherents to weaken a well established govt. so to spread their own area of influence and control.

The most hazardous and difficult step in guerrilla warfare is its initiation. Mao's rebellion first took the form of workers uprisings; these were defeated and almost all rebels were wiped out. He recovered only after he fled to rural areas and adopted the cause of agrarian reforms. He never initiated guerrilla bands from the grassroot level. His skill lay in uniting communist outcast, disloyal national guards, under paid constables and opportunistic bandits in strife torn China. Mao's method in China have spawned a formidable offspring. Thoughout the world politically ustable, illitrate, poverty stricken countries present fertile ground for Communist Revolutionary Warfare.

It is probable that insurgency or guerilla war will flare up in more countries during the next few years. These outbreaks may not be initially inspired, organised or led by local communist, but they will receive the moral support and vocal encouragement of international communism and where possible, expert advice and material support as well.

Guerrilla warfare is governed by general laws of warfare but since it starts with conspiracy, it is also governed by laws uniquely its own. If there exists a spontaneous popular feeling aginst suppresson it may be possible to organise guerrilla warfare or insurgency on the spot. But generally the struggle is begun abroad or in an isolated spot, centred around some known leader fighting for the salvation of people.

### Mao Tse Tung

He was born in Hunan province of central China in 1893. He was the son of peasant farmer who gave the boy an education available to few chinese at that time. After graduating in 1917, he obtained a post in the peking, university, library, where he associated with the Marxist study group. by 1920, he was a convinced communist, determined to rid China of its centuries old social injustices. In 1926, Mao was back in Hunan agitating for land reforms, at considerable risk. At the split between Chiang Kai Shek Nationalist forces and the communist, Mao took to the mountains and was the leader of the famous 6000 miles long march to Shensi province. In the uneasy truce between Nationalist and Communist in the face of the common Japanese enemy, Mao wrote 'Yu Chi Chan' Guerrilla Warfare, the embodiment of his theories, doctrines and experiences of revolutionary guerrilla war.

### Mao's Doctrine

Mao conceived this type of war as passing through a series of merging phases, the first of which is devoted to organisation, consolidation and preservation of regional base area situated in isolated and difficult terrain. The volunteers are trained here and indoctrinated and then the agitators and propagandist are sent forth inidividually or in groups of two or three to persuade and convince the inhabitants of the surrounding country side and to enlist their support. In effect there is thus woven about each base a protective belt of symphathizers, willing to supply food, recruits and information. The pattern of the process is conspiratorial cladestine, methodical and progressive. The operations would be spordic. Because of superior information, insurgents always engage under condition of their own choosing, because of superior knowledge of terrain, they are able to use it to their advantage and security forces discomfiture. Insurgents fight only when the chances of victory are weighted heavily in their favour and if the tide of an operation, go against them, they withdraw. Attacks are sudden, sharp, vicious and short in duration to harnass and demoralize the security forces. In conventional tactics, dispersion of forces invites destruction where as in guerrilla warfare the very tactics is available both to confuse the security forces and to preserve the illusion that guerrilla are ubiquitos. The following fundamental steps are neccessary in developing insurgency.

- Arousing and Gathering Sympathisers and aggrieved population.
- Explaining and convincing them the cause of the movement.
- Establish Bases for organising, training and development.
- Equipping the insurgents for the operational assigments.
- Effective propganda to win support of population and make efforts to come in lime light of the govt.
- Spread area of influence by militant actions
- Gain control of the territory to full fill the cause of the movement.

# 2

# Insurgencies in India: A Re-Capitulation

Conventional wars in the present day changing environment has become rare because of countries acquiring nuclear weapons and fear of conventional warfare escalating into nuclear warfare, always exists. Therefore insurgency, sponsering of guerrilla warfare in the neighbouring countries seems to have become the rule rather than the exception. Under the nuclear umbrella canopy unconventional wars and insurgencies are on an increase, when security forces are round the clock committed in counter insurgency operations. The terrain and the civil population in the area and military situation in the insurgency environment, demand modifying of SF units and sub units to specifically meet the operational requirement of counter insurgency operations. In addition the troops would need specialized training for these operations.

Since 1947, India has fought dozens of insurgent movements like in North East States. Punjab, Jammu & Kashmir and now maoist insurgency in Central India. The insurgencies in North East and Jammu & Kashmir are generally contained but not totally under control, Punjab insurgency stands defeated, but Maoist insurgency which is trying to escalate, needs to be dealt firmly. There are broadly four types of terrorism/insurgencies, one etho-nationalist which focuses on creating a seperate state like the tribal insurgent groups of North East India (known as seven sister states). The second one is religious which is pedominantly sponsered by Pakistan, then the Nacro-terrorism which aims at illigal narcotics trafficing, like the one in North West India. The left wing terrorism focuses mainly on economic ideology through voilent means. Maoist insurgency in Jharkhand and Chhattisgarh are the example of this movement.

The insurgency in North East India has been too tough to deal with and prologed and still erupts at intervals. There are reasons for their survival for too long which mainly are their locations astride International Border and the rugged terrain favouring guerrilla operations. North East is bordered by four countries, China & Bhutan in its North Mynamar on its East and Bangladesh on its South and West. The terrain in North East (NE) where Nagas and Mizos operated is far too rugged, there are impregnable bamboo curtains and deep valleys and escape routes to their camps in the neighbouring countries. Nagas & Mizos in North East utilized this terrain and geography of the land to the fullest extent.

The things that would prove obstacle to an outsider are fully taken advantage of by these insurgents. These insurgents are not mere nomads, but a well worked mechinery of war which could be put into action within no time. Their tactics differes slightly from Maoist insurgents, while in defence they never think it wise to behave like a fanatic and fight till the last. While attacked they always try to throw the enemy back by a determined resistance and if found the attacking troops too strong they would thin out leaving a few men to hold the attacker at bay and then escape to safety. Mobility is their greatest asset. Through their hard enduring life they amidst the rugged terrain surrounding know to befriend the multifarious and ugly postures of nature and treat them as part of life. The location of the villages on hill tops are used to advantage from there the process of heligraphy is also brought into play and information is passed through prearranged signals like torch lights, burning of fire to indicate impending danger of Security Forces (SFs). Bird calls and drum beats are also used as means of communication and passing of information. Therefore it is equally important for the SFs operating in these areas to assimilate these conditions which favour locals.

North East states are connected to India by Siliguri corridor which is 23 Kms in width. Nagaland was created in 1963 as the 16th state of India from Assam State. The Naga National Council led by Phizo was the first group to dissent in 1947 and in 1957 they went underground and other groups also picked this and joined insurgent movement. There are large number of ethnic groups with different languages and dialects. The broad racial difference with India is due to its geographical location ie Siliguri corridor which gives a sense of alienation to them and ultimately rose to a political culture of violent seperatism. Some of their ethnic groups are looking for total independence, other for ethnic identities and homeland, whereas some have made it a profession to extort money without any aim or ideology.

The immigration from densely populated Bangladesh which began in 1920s (East Pak), resulting in indigenous ethinic groups getting into minority, has also aggravated the inter group rivalaries. The most important negative impact of these activities has been internal displacement of population. Fear psychosis among the ethnic groups exists due to frequent cases of killing, kidnapping, threat and extortion. Thus a common man suffers. Politics is rendered completely polluted. Nexus between insurgents and politicians has made electoral system a farce. Most of the funds allocated for development are pocketed by insurgents in connivance with the politicians. The Armed Forces Special Power Act (AFSPA) is always a subject with the rebels to provoke the masses, the act which provides certain amount of safeguards to the Security Forces (Army) who are actively involved in counter insurgency operations and often suffer heavy casualties also.

The latest attack by Bodo(s) on the Adivasis in Kokrajhar and Sonitpur destricts of Assam on 23 December 2014, killing nearly 80 innocent people has once against exposed poor state of law and order mechniery. It was in second half of 19th Century that Britishers Tea Planters brought these Adivasis from Chhota-Nagpur and Central India to Assam to work as labourers. Later a second batch of Adivasis came to Western Assam looking for better life. But over the long time nothing has changed for better for the Adivasis. Tea gardens are owned by multinational companies. The marginalized community of Adivasis has become a soft target for insurgent group like BODO. Even Nagas have started troubling these Adivasis. They accuse Adivasis for settling in the area over which Assam and Nagaland both have a claim. BODOs want Non-BODOs to move out of Assam which include Muslims, Christians and Adivasis. In the past also large number of Adivasis were killed in this area and as result some of them took on arms for their safety and formed a few outfits, which though later laid down their arms infront of then Home Minister P. Chidambaram, a few years ago. Security analysts fear that latest attack on Adivasis may provoke them to take up arms again. They may even be swayed by Maoist who have already set up bases close to Arunachal Pradesh. Adivasis also want SC status. Traditionally loyal to congress, these Adivasis have now started moving close to BJP. In 2014 General Elections, out of 14, seven MP seats, BJP won and two of them are 'Adivasis'.

The gruesome killing of innocent Adivasis in December 2014 has been taken very seriously. The Central government of India blame the state govt. for inept handling and ignoring the intelligence inputs about this ghastly incident. They have also asked the Army Unified Command, Head Quarter at Tezpur to firmly deal with these militants. The neighbouring countries Bhutan and Myanmar have also been requested not to let these miscreants find safe heavens in their territory, hopefully these sincere and serious efforts should yeild desired and expected results.

# 3

# Emergence of Maoist Insurgency

Maoist insurgency is an ongoing conflict between Maoist groups also known as Naxalites and Indian government for the last over 45 years. The movement is an offshoot of Maoist movement in Nepal which gradually spread to jungles in the foot hill of West Bengal. It is termed as Naxalite because it began from a village Naxalbari in West Bengal in 1967. The Naxalite movement was basically by aggrieved peasantry of the area which though was quashed around Naxalbari but had escalated to other areas. Naxalites are a group of far left radical communists, supportive of Maoist Communist idealogy. They do not believe in parliamentary democracy and progress and practice path of armed struggle. Though intially the movement started in West Bengal but has now spread into less developed rural areas of Central and East India known as Red Corridor, which affects 28 districts and covers an area of approximately 92,000 Kms. The Maoist insurgents have taken advantage of popular discontent to expand their area of influence.

The difference between Maoist strategy and struggle

and Naxalite movement is that both began from Naxalbari (West Bengal) in 1967. Maoist movement is the outcome of 1967 uprising and they work with an agenda and use of weapons to achieve their aim, whereas Naxals focus on mass organisation, the original spirit of Naxalbari where huge mineral deposits were discoverd in some forested area and government decided to shift some locals which these tribals did not accept, since then the resistance and reapprisal began.

The period between 1950s and 1970s can be termed as the first phase of Maoist movement in India and the period between 1975 to 1990 as the second phase. The second phase had series of splits due to ideological difference in various groups. But still the movement expanded and sympathisers overtly or covertly supported it. The period between 1991-2003 saw consolidation of the insurgent groups People War Group (PWG), Maoist Communist Centre (MCC) and CPI parts came together and emerged as main Maoist front of India. Their aim remains to overthrow democratic government of India and seize power through armed revolution. The arrest of Kobad Ghandy in 2009 revealed that he was engaged with educated people in urban areas to preach Maoist ideology, which included workers in the telecom and power sectors, most of who are migrant labourers.

The conlict in its present form began in 2004 after formation of CPI Maoist, a rebel group consisting of PWG and MCC. In January 2005 talks between Andhra Pradesh and Naxal broke down and since then the conflict has escalated manifolds and has spread in large area. They have raised People Liberation Guerrrilla Army (PLGA), which has increased in strength. The rebels accused Andhra Pradesh govt. for not accepting their demand for written truce, release of prisoners and allocation of land. The PLGA has about

6500-9500 cadre mostly with small arms. They are mostly effective in state of Bihar, Jharkhand, Chhatisgarh and Andhra Pradesh and have support of Adivasis (tribals) of the area. There have been large number of casualty of civilians, SFs and the population displaced due to insurgency. By 1980, it was estimated that around 30 Naxalite groups were active with a total strength of approximentes 30,000 insurgents. The man known as Kishenji was the main architect of Naxal strategy. After his death in November 2011, the insurgency started fading but has started reviving once again.

The hostilities in recent past have been increasing local authorities have failed to contain insurgency and the most affected are the 30 million tribals spread over the red corridor. The death toll upto 2013 as estimated has been as under :-

(a) Security Forces - 2500 (approx)

(b) Civilion Population - 6500 (approx)

(c) Insurgents - 3000 (approx)

Jharkhand is the most affected state as of date. Most of the state govt. has not been able to complete its full tenure. The Adivasis count 26% of the population and depend on forest for the their livelihood, which has been leased by the state govt to various companies. When huge minerals deposits were discovered in some forested area, the govt. shifted large number of population in 1967 to other locations with no proper compensation. The locals felt it was the exploitation and resorted to rebellion which took shape of Maoist insurgency. These Maoist now inhibit area known as Red Corridor that stretches from West Bengal to Karnataka. Their focus is on tribals and lower caste people for support.

The state police employed in these area are poorly trained and has weak leadership to counter the insurgency. The civilian authorities who are resposible in implementing development plans in these areas are not fully motivated for the job. The SFs should also be trained to win the heart and mind of the locals and should ensure no human right violations. The insurgency gained media attention in 2013 Naxal attack in Darba Valley resulting in death of 24 congress leaders. They also killed Mr. Mahendra Karma, Salwa Jadum Founder in an attack while he was compaigning in the area for congress. There is an urgent need for the Indian government to take some pragmatic approach to contain this insurgency in the interest of regional stability. The estimated casualities in Chhatisgarh alone upto December 2014 have been:-

(a) SFs- 830 (Approx)

(b) CiVs - 700 (Approx)

(c) Insurgents - 750 (Approx)

The current approach of the govt. towards finding a worthwhile solution to this menace has not made any worthwhile headway. Use of excessive force like Cobera and Operation Green Hunt to wipe out insurgents has also generally failed. The insurgency has been fading and reviving time and again. The govt. is trying to go after their leaders, which brings on a temporary peace. The ambush laid by the insurgents on 6 April 2010, killing 76 personnel of CRPF, patrol party was a big blow to our military operations and a big moral booster for the insurgents. CRPF which is operating against, the insurgent are not trained in counter insurgency operations and they are deficient of required equipment and other logistic support. They have to cover vast area in hostile terrain where they have to move on foot, without bullet proof jackets, equipment to deal with IEDS, night vision devices and thermal sensors etc. They are even defficient of manpower to cover and dominate the vast area of Red Corridor. These problems need to be addressed on priority by the government so that the insurgent do not take advantage of our weakness once again.

The efforts of state and central government need to be integrated to deal with this menace. The success of Andhra Pradesh to curb insurgency can not only be attributed to security force alone, it was dealt with by increasing presence of govt in the areas where naxalites had established their authority due to vaccum. They also trained their police force well, spread their intelligence network, during the period of ceasefire and the results have been commendable.

# 4

# Maoist Idealogy & Strategy to Expand Their Area of Influence

The Naxalites in India are associated with CPI (Maoist). They are considered far left radical communists supportive of Maoist political sentiments & ideology. The origin can be traced to the split in 1967 of the CPI (marxist) leading to formation of CPI (marxist lennist). Initially the movement had its centre in West Bengal and then spread to less developed rural areas through group like CPI (maoist).

## Mao's Ideology

Terrorism/insurgency in an anxiety inspiring method of repeated voilent action employed by clandestime individual groups or state actors for criminal or political reasons for which targets are the population which works as message generator. Maoist concept of insurgency is to teach the people carefully planned manouvers and certain other techniques such as the amount of force required is small, but if it is applied scientifically for the greatest effect, it can be difficult to overcome. Mao advocated first to employ inferior force, both in number and in the quality of trained, desciplined and few weapons, but he fought when he had the advantage. In Mao's theory of war there is no disgrace in running away since mobility and surprise are his important ingredients. Mao's frist and foremost principle of guerrilla warfare, is the civil action war, which is ultimately won or lost in the minds of people. The communist insist on an attitude of strict descipline, honesty and friendly cooperation towards the people and all military operations must further political objectives. Every period of military inactivilty must be used to further communist indoctrination of the guerrilla themselves and of the people. Intelligence is important but comes mostly from the people. Mao realized that inherently guerrilla would be less well-armed and equipped than adversaries, but he saw no great disadvantage in this. The equipment of the guerrilla can not be based on what the guerrilla want or even what they need, but must be based on what is available, more could be acquired gradually.

Mao advocated first stage to establish bases within civil population and second to take on guerrilla warfare operations like ambushes and surprise attacks and third stage to go on to conventional warfare.

How does Mao's plan works is yet to be seen. 1950-53 Korean War appears to have put an end to communist expansion, but menace is likely to continue at low level for sometime. The fragmenting of communist world has lent credence to the arguement that communists advance by proxy, as is attempted by them is only of peripheral importance due to weakening rigid central control of the communists.

Insurgency does not emerge in isolation. Its underlying causes are invariably to be found in political, social, economic, religious domains and other demands of people.

The Naxalite-Maoist insurgency is a long drawn conflict. These insurgents are fighting for the betterment of the poor people of the area. They demand more jobs and improvment in the living conditions of the tribals. They feel a gross injustice has been done by the govt by ignoring the demands of the masses.

Maoists have adopted new strategy that include mass attack and hit and run tactics and they quickly shift operational bases. They primarily attack govt and police personnel. According to the institute of peace and conflict studies, Naxal group have recruited children in different capacities and expose them to danger. They have been consolidating their gains and spreading to new areas, steadily improving their military capabilities and tactics. They also carryout maticulous planning, good preparation, good, effective and result oriented execution. Naxalites extort huge sum of money from corporators, mine owners forest and Public Works Contractors, businessmen, land lords and corrupt officials. Maoists rebels are illigally mining and selling coal from the coalfieds, owned by Coal India Ltd and they are using this money to promote insurgency.

The insurgents recruit young local boys, who are indoctrinated and then given military training. They are given individual and group tasks involving great endurance and leadership. Alongwith continues the training in toughening up and art of warfare including use of weapons, ambush, raids etc. Rigid descipline, strict obedience, limitless endurance and faith in the goodness of the cause which is supposed to have all religious and moral sanctions. Surprise and deception are the important part of their tactical doctrine. The insurgents lay emphasis on laying ambushes while dealing with the Security Forces (SFs), because against an organised military force, it proves an effective instrument.

Before laying an ambush the insurgents always ensure the tactical soundness of the plan. Generally the areas selected for an ambush meet all the tactical prerequisites of a good site and all the drills are rehearsed before actual execution and proper escape routes are chosen. The ambush parties are very well organised with proper strength and proper weapons, required to ambush the patrolling party of SFs.

Their tactics involves total annihilation of the patrolling group, snatching away the weapons of the dead and quickly thin out and disappear in the jungle. In 2013, Maoist developed a new tactics in their warfare of booby trapping of dead bodies of soldiers with Improvised Explosive Devices (IEDs) in their bodies.

The Maoist insurgency is gaining momentum in Jharkhand and some other parts of Central India. Of late the banned CPI (Maoist) is also, eying fertile ground for showing their presence in three districts of Kerala ie Malappuram, Palakkad and Wayanad. They try to exploit popular sentiments against environmental pollution caused by and querrying activities, exploitation of natural resources, alleged high headedness of police and forest officials and displacement of tribals due to tourism products and wild life sanctuaries. Some of the activities are serious cause of worry for the govt for Kerala getting in the list of left wing extremist, maoist (CPI).

When we analyse the tactics of an insurgent, we see that the insurgent must possess a highly developed knowledge of the terrain on which he operates, avenues of access and escape, possibilities of rapid manoevure, popular support and hiding places. All this favours rural area. Moreover here the insurgent can represent the desires of poor tribals who support them in their cause whole heartedly. Insurgency is basically fight of the people for liberation. Thus the essence of insurgency is the miracle by which a small band of people, looking beyond their immediate tactical objectives become Vanguard of a mass movement, achieving its ideals establishing a new force to win social justice. Insurgency basically derives from the masses and is supported by them, it can neither exist nor flourish if it separates itself form their sympathies and cooperation. They have a particular political aim and goal, without which the insurgency will fail, since the popular support will be lacking without political objectives which should come with the aspirations of people.

The insurgent basically spring from the masses of people who may initially suffer for lack of proper organisation and proper leadership. Since the cause is common, they flourish faster and find their, way soon. Once they find a leader who is unyielding, resolute, loyal, sincere and robust and is able to organise and establish strict discipline, he becomes a model for them to follow. Insurgency is the method of warfare of the weaker side. Therefore they will analyse in detail the CI force operations, manpower, popular support, weapons and leadership and then plan their strategy to confront these factors, keeping in mind their final aim of distablising a well established govt, against whose misgovernance, they have grievances.

# 5

# Peculiarities of Insurgency Operations and Special Training Needed to Counter Insurgency

Specific terrain, internal situation and political environment in the area of counter insurgency operations require modifying of convention Force for operation against the insurgents. In addition to modifications they need specialized training before they are launched as part of a counter insurgency campaign.

The casualities of Para Military Force (CRPF) are more in Maoist insurgency compared to Jammu & Kashmir or North East States. Maoists have acquired good technology of devising and planting explosives (IEDs) in these areas. Since most of them are local, know the area well which help them in laying effective ambush and resulting in mass killings of SFs. High intensity conflict zones look less affected casualty wise then Maoist bastions of Jharkhand, Chhatisgarh and Odisha, today. In April 2010, CRPF patrol suffered 76 personnel killed in an ambush in Dantewala.

Before the troops are moved to the area of operation, it is imparative to stress on them the need for such an operation and necessity of their active participation. All ranks of the SFs must be made aware of fundamental requirement of winning the minds and heart of the people and of the ways in which this can be done and by whom. They should also be firmly conveyed what not to do. They should be told that local population is the most important ally of the insurgents. These locals provide food, shelter, intelligence, medical care and the manpower (recruits) etc. The local also deny informations about insurgent identity and location of their training camps etc. Hence the SFs can not hope to succeed in counter insurgency operations if they alienate the local population Local population can be won over by various civic actions and by working in close lion with the civil administration. If the insurgent is to be eliminated, he must be excluded from the village life, otherwise he can escape any offensive pressure by going quiescent. Every inhabitant spot must be subject to permanent surveillance so that existance of any stranger becomes difficult. This can best be achieved with the help of local agents, informer and police.

The terrain where insurgency breeds, mostly poses navigational and communication problems and the weather in these jungles and hilly terrain is conducive to the generation of mosquitoes, leeches and many other insects. Troops need to be trained and educated to guard against these health hazards while involved in active insurgency. The insurgents generally being locals prove to be versatile to whom tactics were dictated by his instinct and inherited knowledge of the terrain and jungle craft. They utilize the terrain and geography of the land to the fullest extent. The ground aspect that would prove obstacle to conventional security forces is taken full advantage by the insurgents.

The area with jungle, steep hills, nullahs etc greatly reduce the visibility and make communication, particularly during monsoons a dreadful affair. The insurgents generally refrain from fighting a pitched battle and act in small groups, looking for suitable targets.

Physical toughness of the counter insurgency force also gains added importance since the nature of the terrain and tactics usually restrict the use of conventional means of mobility, forcing counter insurgency force to move on foot. Thus to outmatch the mobility of the insurgents, the CI force needs to be really tough only then can they give the elusive insurgents a chase to keep them on the run and eventually capture them.

The insurgent are generally recruited locally. They have the intimate knowledge of the ground and they use this to their full advantage in operations particularly for achieving mobility and surprise. Therefore there is a need for the CI force to acquire detailed knowledge of their area of operation, which can be gained through extensive patrolling and close liaison with the locals, which though is time consueming process. Once this is achieved it will give good amount of confidence to the troops in their counter insurgency operations. Endeavour should be, not to turn over trained troops very quickly from the insurgency area.

Gaining information about the insurgents is a slow and difficult process. The normal conventional methods do not prove useful at most of the times. CI force has to heavily depend on civil intelligence agencies for the intelligence inputs hence their liaison with them has to be good. Infact there should be a joint intelligence centre for exchange of intelligence. The locals such as local forest guards, informers etc are good source of intelligence gathering. Even heliborne patrolling for visual recce prove very useful at times. The intelligence has to be fool proof, sence faulty and false intelligence input may prove fatal in operations.

In counter insurgency operations, capture of a piece of ground has no significance. CI tactics therefore aims at seek, harrass and destroy the insurgents which vastly differs from conventional warfare tactics. The insurgent should get the feel of being hunted and isolated, this will not permit them time to reorganise and rest. Once a significant insurgent force is located, maximum force should be applied to liquidate it.

Emphasis should be laid on training for immediate action drills like countering an ambush, raid or to counter a local action by the insurgent groups. Due to lack of proper and well coordinated training our CI force have at times suffered heavy casualties in the operations against well motivated and trained insurgents. Counter insurgency operations are different since location and direction of the impending danger can not be predicted. Most of the actions would be at subunit level. Proper indoctrination and proper toughness ensure better operational efficiency. Initiative, boldness and aggressiveness on part of junior leaders pay very handsome dividents in counter insurgency operations.

Patrolling is very important aspect of CI operations which forms major portion of the activities. The patrol team should be trained as per the requirement of the terrain and insurgents tactics. Each man knows his job and performs it well. The nature of each mission is such that any member of the team can be placed in command. Every team member therefore must know the nature and the purpose of the mission, including infiltration, exfiltration routes of travel, escape routes, details of supporting elements, call signs and the time plan. The time allotted will depend on the nature of the mission and type of terrain. Sometimes we tend to become casual and overlook important aspect that route in and out of the patrol should never be the same. Our troops have suffered heavy casualties while taking the same route on the way back and were ambushed by the insurgents. This reflects adversly on the execution of CI operations and such criticism leaves little room for complacency. Though the performance of the CI force may have been commendable in the past, but to meet the future challenges one has to do better.

Where possible plan two to three column, moving on parallel lines, this would give advantage of distracting and dispersing the insurgents and ultimately fullfilling the tasks of area familiarisation and domination/surveilliance. It would also help presenting a small target to the ambushing party of the insurgents. The insurgents know the fatigue level of the returning patrol party and sense of slackness creeps in when they are nearing their camp area, this is the most vulnerable time and place for the SFs for attack or ambush by the insurgents.

Soldiers involved in CI operations have short term view and their tactical operations have short term immediate aim. In this short term, aim should also be to win over the local, so that one knows and gains the intelligence about the insurgents. This aim can only be done with the full support of the govt. like building roads, schools and hospitals etc and also by providing them protection and being kind to them. It is well known fact that wherever their grievances are real, only then the trouble erupts and insurgents and locals join as one group. This group will always be alienated from their govt. or else why should the security force be asked to intervene. It is for this reason that locals can not be easily separated from the insurgents.

Another very important aspect in all spheres of group

activities is sound leadership. This gains added importance when faced with danger to own life and that of his group. In the context of military force particularly, if leader is not sound and capable, its effect could be seen on his combat team. Leadership is the process of influencing individual and his organisation. In combat it is more important since each level leaves a certain area of discretion to the level below.

Even the last soldier exercises some measure of judgement in determining his specific action in a particular situation. When the lowest ranking soldier is considered, it is apparent that a great variety of influences operate to determine his actions. He is mostly influenced more and more by his training, motivation, moral and trust in each other to support in crisis in the face of the enemy. This can not be supervised and guided by the leader on the spot in active encounter with the insurgents. The criterion of effective leadership is the quality of performance demonstrated by the troops in combat under his command. Flexibility in active operations is related to the leaders personality, his experience, his competence and the situation. Personal rigidity, lack of experience and training and similar impediments may restrict his capacity in on the spot decision making to get out of the crisis.

In insurgency, the command of all the military activities must be centralized in one person of each level of command in the heirarchy. The top leader must pass his instructions directly to the next echelon of his subordinates all the way down. At every level in the chain the commander must direct operations in his area. As regards other advisers involved in CI operations are concerned, their advice would help formulate a sound operational plan and commander decision making. The risk of success of operations, policies and priorities, selection of targets, allocation of resources, all fall within the ambit of top commanders charter of responsibilities.

In insurgency enemy is generally from within and encounters are carried out in the interior of the country. The move of small force in jungle or broken terrain becomes difficult and dangerous for any moment the march may become an engagement with the insurgents. The ability to run away after strike is the very characteristic of the insurgents. Therefore the CI force should be capable of detecting the insurgent and temporarily neutralizing them, to capture or liquidate them. In this type of terrain, aviation except for reece, casualty evacuation and some logistic support is of not much use. APC or armour has no space for menouvre. These are only the hand grenades and machine guns, which prove of real value. In present day maoist insurgency, the fundamental principle in conducting operations against our own lawless people is to sieze and retain initiative and domination of the affected area.

# 6

# Political Environment in India to Curb Insurgency

India is both challenging and frustrating, challenging because of its promise and frustrating because of its performance. It suffers from escalating overpopulation, from too much emphasis on industralization and not enough on agriculture and too much reliance on government enterprise instead of private enterprises. Many are still not too hopeful about its required development. The present leadership of India is at least trying to bring in changes and development all around. The overpopulated nation with meagre resources in seeking ways to wrench itself forward in exceedingly difficult circumstances. Government needs to shift its means and adjust its institutions so that planned objectives can be more quickly and more effectively achieved. People in broad sense have become an entity to be served rather than used for development. What matters is the government sincere efforts in consciously delibrated and pragmatically developing in the direction of great liberty, greater abundance, broader choice and increased popular involvement in the processes of the government whether that process in going to proceed at the pace fast enough to keep our steps ahead of the pressure of rising expectations is one of the great questions and challenges of the years ahead.

India is staggering giant and any discussion on Asia future must ultimately focus on the respective roles of four giants. India the most populous non- communist developing nation, Japan, Asia's principal industrial and economic power, China the world's most populous, developing and Asias most immediate threat and U.S. the greatest pacific power. Though U.S.S.R. occupies much of the land map of Asia, its principal focus is towards the West and its vast Asian lands are an appendage of European Russia.

One of the major causes of brewing insurgencies in India is poor development in remote areas which lacks even the basic emenities. In these areas one still notices women squatting in the mud, forming cow dung patties with her hand and laying them out to dry, while a transistor radio in her lap plays local music. It will need concentrated efforts on part of the government to bring visions of the future to these remote tribal villages which are credible and achievable. Too wide a gap between reality and expectation always produces an explosive situation and fact that whatever leadership knows is possible, is unknown to great mass of the peasantry. If the leadership knows what is possible to achieve should be done.

Most of the developing countries vary widely in their social traditions and political systems but their methods of economic, management have certain traits in common ie prime reliance on private enterprises and on pricing mechanism of the market as the chief determinant of the business decisions, a pacing of monetary expansion to match growth in output, receptivity to private capital investment, both domestic and foreign, including such incentives as tax advantage and quick government clearance of proposal of the projects, imaginative national programmes for dealing with social problems and not the least, a generally restrained posture in government planning, with government role being suggestive rather than coersive.

India has large number of insurgent groups operating across the country, reflecting an acute sense of alienation on part of the people involved. Wikipedia list 16 belligerent groups and 68 organisations as terrorist groups in India, which include mine in North East four in centre and East includings Maoist (Naxals), 17 in the West (Sikh Separatist groups) and 38 in Jammu & Kashmir. The seven states of the North East (NE) are different ethnically and linguistically from rest of India. Their demand is mostly for a separate state and autonomy. They also blame the central government for neglecting them in issues of education, poverty and lack of economic opportunities. Assam has ULFA and National Democratic Front BODO (NDFB), major insurgent groups. Meghalaya has a problem of devide between tribals and non-tribals settlers. Arunachal Dragon Force also demands an independent state. Mizoram problems has been mainly due to domination of Assamese and neglect of Mizos by the central government. Nagaland which came into being in 1963 happens to be the oldest insurgency since 1947 and are demanding independent state. It is this move which has given impetus to other groups in the adjoining states. Tripura has a problem due to Bengali immigrants and Manipur also feels neglected and demand independence. Insurgency in Punjab is totally under Control where- as in Jammu & Kashmir, it is Pak sponsered terrorism from accross the border and is an on going conflict and being effectively dealt with by the Army.

The type of population mix due to migrants from all

over, India has never been a homogenous society. The multiplicity of races, ethnicity, tribes, religion and language led to internal problems. Indian caste system divides the people into potential conflict segments. In addition large number of population is poor, living under poverty line, lacking most of the basic necessities.

In Bihar the 'Ranvir Sena' comprising of upper cast landlords were accused of killing Dalits in the pretext of Maoist insurgency. There are also other small insurgent groups which have also emerged ie, Red Tigers, Green Tigers etc. In Chhattisgarh Salwa Jadum an anti insurgency operation was launched to counter insurgency in 2005. This consisted of local tribals, trained by state government as alleged by the maoist. National Human Right Commission who investigated the allegations found that these youths of Salwa Judum got fed up of maoist activities and took up arms voluntarily against them.

Over the years rebels have launched series of attacks on security forces. The government has decided to crack down even harder untill insurgents renounce violence and enter peace talks. The government has sent about 81000 para military force in these areas called 'Green Hunt' which has further worsened the position and Adivasis are more, and more taking on arms. Though the insurgents have been pushed back deep into the jungles but they carryout hit and run tactics.

In Assam a major break through in the center's crackdown on National Democratic Front of Bodoland(s) faction, the outfil behind the massacre of 78 people on Assam in December 2014, has greatly debilitated NDFB(s) which has been resisting talks and indulging in wanton Killings of tribals across Kokrajhar, Sonitpur, Chirang and Baksa areas.

With the known strength of NDFB to be around 260-280 and with the killing of three senior commanders and arrest of 58 cadres, is described as a crippling blow to the outfit. The centre has also deployed an additional SSB Battalion to seal off border in the event of NDFB(s) cadres attempting to flee to Bhutan.

The use of conventional Para Military Force to overcome insurgency in combat is relatively a minor requirement in the defeat of an insurgency. The political action, psychological and social support of populace for the subverted authority therefore is the major requirement for counter insurgency success. The insurgent uses tactics and equipment not to defeat the SFs he opposes, but to render it insufficient and incapable of leadership and security for the sovereignty it supports. His objectives are psychological but his means may be military. Insurgency and terrorism are political matters and that politics can only be handled by the local civil authorities.

State of Andhra Pradesh has been able to control the menace of maoist insurgency and as a result maoist hardly were able to mount attacks and the casualty of SFs between 2008 and 2013 has just been three. Though latest intelligence input suggest maoist regrouping to take advantage of the devision of the state looking for an opportunity to resurrect themselves in an uncertain administrative atmosphere. Given that a majority of CPI (maoist) leadership comes from Telangana, the desire to resurrect Maoism in the State has always been there with the outfit. The situation as on date is not alarming since the state mechninary has been able to reach the most remote corners of the state leaving little chance for Maoist to stir up passions once again.

# 7

# Government Measures Needed to Defeat Insurgency

The government counter insurgency tactics and strategy has remained generally conservative and traditional, which does not yield the desired result since the insurgent do not attach importance to holding of ground. Naxal corridor is much more difficult for operations than the other insurgency areas and involves high risk of lives of the soldiers. The government therefore should realize the futility of a peice meal approach in fighting Naxalites. There should be coordinated counter operation in all the affected states by plugging all the escape route of maoists. Otherwise these insurgents will keep shifting to safer places in the neighbouring countries/states.

The government needs to be more adept at both using trained force and ensuring visible deployment in these areas. There are two views about tackling of this menace of insurgency, one recommend use of military force to quash them and the other is that since insurgent exploit the sentiments of impoverished locals our attention therefore be focussed more on development. It therefore emerges that combined approach of development and use of force to contain spread of insurgency is the best option. The popularity of Naxalites may reduce if people in the rebel areas get basic amenities such as roads, water, schools and hospitals etc. The state anti-naxalite police force needs to be better trained, equipped and better paid. Picking up more locals, who know the terrain better will pay handsome dividend. The civil servant in these areas should be motivated and keen to address local problems. Till such time government servants at grassroot level do not ensure implementation of government policies of providing basic amenities which are the cause of conflict, no headway to resolve the issue can be made. It is rightly said that security without development in questionable, while development in insurgency, without security is impossible. The underlying causes of insurgency are invariably found in political, socio-economic or religious fields.

So far government response has not been very good both at policy formulation and execution level. Though the government announced nation wide initiative in February 2009 which was termed as Integrated Action Plan. This included grassroot economic development projects in naxalite affected areas. The affect of these were positive and the insurgency was on decline and as a result of improved situation Karnataka was taken off the list of affected states in 2010. However the spurt of offensive in 2013 by the insurgents made the situation grim one again. The insurgents have started extorting money from active entrepreneurs operating in the area. This money is extensively used to finance their operations in the area.

The government have generally failed to find effective

solution to the insurgency problem and has attempted piece meal plans. The civilian administration are too concerned with the trivia of law enforcement and anyway look inwards at their own people, ie businessmen, politician, statesmen, all are committed in their mundane tasks or are excluded by partisan interests or security doubts. Though their activities in anycase are essential part of the life of the community. The government should pay more attention to some of the following issues.

- Instead of involving in large scale operations, we must target on it leadership since insurgents do not hold permanent ground, hence use of conventional force does not effectively work.

  Personal interest, of local politicians should not restrict their legitimate actions and vote bank politics should be avoided.

- There should be strict and serious move to crackdown on the corrupt machinery in the state, who are mostly responsible in not letting the benefit of various government plan go down to the affected lot of the population.
- Effort should be made to ensure law and order in the affected areas with help of village elders. Because there can not be stability before development and development can only be undertaken when environment is condusive and peaceful.
- The state police in the area of insurgency remain weakened by skill crisis and weak and de-motivated leadership. Attention should be paid to overcome this serious issue, otherwise states dependence on outside support of SFs would continue.

To combat insurgency a permanent and uniform pattern of action must be developed. In the first or preventive phase vigilance and detection take priority. The intelligence organisations need to increase their efficacy in exchange of information and in actually infiltrating the insurgent groups. By working among the subversives in their own environment, task of suppression will be simplified.

The insurgent first need to be separated from the civilians otherwise it will become difficult to defeat them. It is also believed that the persistant existence of an insurgent movement is something like a plebiscite indicating a broad support for and a kind of legitimacy of the movement in question. Insurgents need popular support in order to survive, therefore those who survive are popular. The government therefore should first endeavour to deny this popular support to the insurgents by addressing the problems which have led to the prevailing situation. Insurgency would fail it its political objectives do not co-incide with the aspiration of the people and their sympathy, co-operation and assistance can not be gained.

When we analyse the tac of the insurgents, we see that he must possess a highly developed knowledge of the terrain on which he operates, avenues of access and escape, possibility for rapid maneouvre, popular support and living places. They also need a strategic location, secure base area for training, self preservation and development. Mobility and surprise are also the key elements in the insurgent strategy.

Geography is always a determining factor in insurgency operations. The insurgent is interested primarily in the weakening and overthrowing of a legitimate government. His area of influence in governed more by the consideration of population activities potential. The insurgency actions are being kept from being capricious only by revolution-social, political and economic which inspires the insurgency from the outset. Insurgent combat activity in all cases has an objective which transcends military accomplishment. Enlightened by a system of action oriented ideas, the organised insurgents fight to undermine established authority, to erode its popular support and to change the social order in his area of responsibility.

The MFs involved in CI operations require intense physical and theoritical training courses of instructions. These must be developed in the geo and climatical orientation as well as tactical survival in the type of terrain obtaining in the CI operations. In our Maoist insurgency it is mostly the CRPF (PMF) which is involved in CI operations. The involvement of Army as some may feel, will not be prudent in this context for its is already heavily committed on borders of our country, and may not be in the overall interest of the government and that of the army to fight own youth and tribals. The Army is already imparting training in CI operations to the selected commanders of the PMFs who can in turn pass it on to their rank and file to be fully trained to fight insurgency. NSG has started heliborne (HB) operation training to CRPF in slithering to enhance their skill in anti maoist operations. The fleet of MI-17 helicopters deployed for anti maoist operations are being used by black cat. Some Un-Armed Vehicles (UAV) can also be provided by IAF. Logistic support, casualty evacuation, transportation support are already being provided by IAF.

The training should also be followed by psychological instructions to give the troops firm conviction on the reasons for the operations. They need to understand its place in a free and democratic society and the fundamental values they are defending. As regards re-organisation of sub unit into proper tactical groups to counter the insurgent tactic may also need a relook. This may be necessitated due to constant improvement in weapons and training the maoist insurgents get from hostile neighbour countries. In the actual operational scenario many factors will vary with almost every situation and off the battlefield a valid basis for test in difficult to define. There is one proven test of time. A few efficient individuals arms tactics and political techniques supplied by outside sponsors to insurgents have made present insurgency more formidable.

The insurgents need a base for rest, training and recoup, otherwise they can not survive as a force. It is therefore important for the MFs to not let them establish camps in the area of operations and deny them safe sanctuaries. The force that allows the grace to the insurgents are either incompetent or insufficient for the assigned task. The national leadership should also take action to ensure that these insurgent do not find sanctuaries in the neighbouring countries also.

# 8

# Potential of Maoist Insurgency in India

Guerrilla warfare is thousands of years old and from Bibalical times through Soviet resistance to Germans in World War II, these conflicts were similar. But those fought in South East Asia Since 1945 have been quite different and Chinese Communist leader Mao Tse Tung has been largely responsible for the changes. It is fundamentally different from the wars of the past and has been called revolutionary war, subversive war or simply modern war. The new type of warfare consist largely the impact which agents of communists subversion can develop at all levels of human activity, political, economic, intellectual, psychological and military with an idea in mind of overthrowing present government and replacing them by other which they consider to have correct political orientation.

Properly organised guerrilla force is an intangible vapour which presents few, if any worthwhile target to sophisticated weapons system. The Chinese description of US as a 'Paper Tiger' is probably based on this part of belief that sophisticated weapons are ineffective against guerrilla and insurgents or subversive forces. Throughout the world the guerrilla warfare has already proved to be well suited to this age of limited warfare under the umbrella of an awesome nuclear deterrent. China has exploited guerrilla war as a corner stone of national strategy.

It is certainly hard to take decision of such intricate problems which involve security, economy and politics. Counter Insurgency aim is to harass seekout and destroy the insurgents and therefore it differs from tactics of conventional warfare. The basic requirement is to arrest the initiative from the insurgents and give them feeling of being isolated and hunted.

The tactics of insurgents involves generally independent operations at lower level for which even supply system is decentralized. All are mostly self reliant and capture of enemy stocks are counted as asset. They bank upon heavily on the popular support and do not get involved into protracted battles. Surprise, Speed and Mobility are the key ingredient of the insurgent tactics and survival. Their weaponry and equipment has also improved. Today they have rocket launchers, mines, booby traps and VHF sets for effective communication.

Maoist Philosophy advocates Power through the barrel of the gun. They do not have belief in Parliamentary democracy and want to usher the New Democratic Revolution (NAR). Their plan involves to build up bases in rural and remote areas which will eventually be transformed into guerrilla zones and later into liberated areas. In order to seize political power by overthrowing the democratically established govt, they believe in protracted mass armed struggle ultimately their planning involves to expand liberated areas and go on for urban areas to seize power.

The maoist insurgency has mostly travelled down from Nepal where it flourished and at one time no political institution were left in Nepal, which have now to a large extent been restored. Indias position is that stability of Nepal rests on two pillars of democracy and constitutional monarchy and at no cost democracy is to be undermined. India concern are most affected by the maoist insurgency. The open border allows maoists access with impunity to anywhere in India. The cross border movement of maoist and arms are another threatening development.

It is now also a known fact that Pak ISI has established some links with maoist to supply them arms and ammunation with the aim to caryout anti India activities from these bases. According to reliable sources the sizeable arsenal of the maoist insurgents consist of weapons of Pak, China and Russia makings in addition to India made, which are mostly taken away from dead bodies of SFs, RPF and loot in Police Stations. It should therefore be well understood by the government that these maoist insurgents who are consolidating their gains and enhancing their capabilities with the help of Pak ISI etc will not desist from carrying out mass killings and destruction of government properties. Marxist style revolution as the maoist appeal to certain section of Indian Society, who are poor, unemployed, exploited by the industrialist with no proper rehabilitation and of course victims of mal-governance, are having a positive response to their preaching.

The root cause of Naxalite maoist insurgency is that the government is not willing to enforce the land ceiling act because it will take away the land from the upper caste land lords who have high stake in the state government. Infact government has failed to implement schedule 5 & 6 of the Indian constitution pertaining to forest and land ceiling respectively. The endgame in the battle against maoist insurgent is yet to begin in right earnest by the government which is very important for overall security of the infested areas. Though at this stage it is not easy to wipe out maoist movement in-one go because it has escalated due to government apathy and arrogance towards poor tribals Though government has announed some projects for these areas, but it is not likely to lure the maoists so soon and easily since the maoist insurgents have started enjoying the extortion money in the mineral rich Chhattisgarh where several businessmen have set up power plants. The state police in most of the insurgency infested area are weakened by skill crisis, weak leadership and shortage of manpower and training to fight the Naxal tactics. The civil servants are not motivated or trained for the kind of job involved in counter insurgency operations.

The tribals in the 'Red Corridor' do not understand the real agenda behind protracted people war, but their living conditions despite the government claims has not improved at all. They have not yet been compensated for the land taken away from them as per the safeguards provided in the constitution for tribal rights. These tribals suffer from both ends ie. SFs and Maoist insurgents. The insurgents torture and kill them by branding them as police informers etc. whereas SFs hold them up and arrest them for providing food, water and shelter to the insurgents. These tribals even complain of threats from corporate security perosonnel. Though the government has pumped millions into various projects in these areas but the nexus between corrupt politicians and civil servants does not let this money be used for the purpose it is meant for. There is therefore need for political reforms and rooting out corruption from the state machinery.

Government at one point felt happy seeing the

dwindling number of the insurgents. The Naxalites also suffered a setback with the arrest of their main leader 'Kabud Ghandy' who was trying to increase influence of the Naxalites in urban areas also. The government should not ignore the active support by China to the maoist insurgent groups in providing sophisticated weapons; the active support of North East insurgents can also not he ruled out. These maoist insurgents are also not short of finances which they conveniently manage through drug, ransom, looting, extortion and poppy crops. These maoists are also trying to infiltrate into educational institution in NCR like JNU etc. to spread their ideologies. Efforts are seriously on to manipulate media coverage favourably by winning their sympathy.

Maoist insrugents at places in Jharkhand are trying to apply Taliban tactics of threatening ladies and girls to dress up as per their dress code. Hand written messages, warning girls, appeared on the walls of the educational institutes. This is done by an unknown groups "Jharkhand Mukti Sangh". They also threatened local social workers and contractors engaged in various projects on behalf of central and state government for the welfare of local population. Some of the contractor, it is learnt have stopped paying the insurgent, hence they are feeling desperate.

Maoist movement in India is a marginal move mainly in tribal and low populated areas and by now has got nowhere much. Still to overcome Naxalites insurgency the government needs to be more adept at both using force and spreading development. The government so far has not made much headway in combining the two factors to produce a workable long term strategy. The battle is being fought by untrained and inefficent police force, which instead of controlling and liquidating the maoist insurgents, has allowed them to spread in other areas too. Though Andhra Pradesh has been able to control the maoist insurgency by combining effort of force and development. The following actions need to be taken immediately to curb the spread of maoist insurgency, to some extent.

- The state anti-naxalite force should be better trained, well paid and well armed to fight this insurgency. Local youth should preferably be recruited in the police force who know the terrain, language and the causes of conflict.

- The state have very little capacity to fight such insurgents as seen in few encounters in the past. Raising additional police force, unless trained and organised on the lines of proper CI force like Assam Rifles etc. will be of not much help and would add additional financial burden on the state.

- CRPF (PMF) which is mostly involved in countering maoist insurgency is also not specialized for this operation since they are called for various assignments at short notice all over, thus they fail to gain expertise in one game. There should be proper re-orientation training for them for CI operations before induction and they should be allowed some fixed time to stay in the area to produce results.

- The policy of option of surrender by government is also good. In 2014 it showed good results since it is very demoralizing for the rebel leadership. The state government should also adopt better psychological warfare including showing good treatment to the surrendered ones and good rehabilitation policy.

- Schedule 5 requires tribal management of forest produce and schedule 6 of land ceiling act. Government should pay attention to this aspect on priority.

# 9

# Urbanisation of Insurgency-An Impending Danger

All over the world, in both developed and under developed countries, the urban areas are increasingly becoming the focus of national activity. The link between urban and rural unrest is also becoming more apparent as poor farmers, victims of modernisation, drift into cities and focus on unemployed slum dwellers, who are highly vulnerable to the lures of the subversive elements of the society. Any type of urban warfare has always presented a unique and dangerous problem. The law, concepts, weapons associated with normal hostilities can be rendered ineffective when an attempt is made to rid the city of a guerrillas or insurgents without destroying the urban complex in the process. Although guerrilla warfare or insurgencies is as old as war, but these have mostly been rural unconventional warfare. This however does not give any overwhelming priority to rural revolution now, nor does it mean that guerrilla warfare can not be applied to cities. In actuality the principles of unconventional warfare can be applied to an urban environment with both validity and a reasonable chance for success.

Important Pre-requistes for Insurgency to Flourish in Urban Areas are given in succeeding text.

**Popular Support**: It is important for an insurgency to be successful. As per Mao Tse Tung "Because guerrilla warfare basically derives from masses and is supported by them, it can neither exist nor flourish if it separates itself from their sympathies and cooperation". Given the discontented masses in our cities, it seems reasonable to assume that a guerrilla force whose objectives are in concert with a significant number of people in a city, could easily obtain popular support.

**Favourable Terrain**: The insurgents or guerrillas need a favourable and familiar terrain to operate. When we analyse the tactics of insurgency operations, it is utmost important for the insurgents to have full knowledge of the terrain, avenues of access and escape, possibilities of rapid manouvre and hides. The buildings in a modern city provide enough scope to meet their tactical requirements.

**Camp Area**: There is a requirement to have a stratigically located camp for training, self preservation and development. It is difficult to find such an area in a city as is available in the country side. However, some feel that it may not be required, if guerrilla remain inactive for some time in a city. But for a prolonged operation necessity of a base area would arise and that can be met by a tie between the city and country side. It is very difficult to establish a secure base in the city, which can be offset to some extant by mixing in the populas and remain inactive in order to rest and regroup.

**Supplies**: The need of guerrilla force can adequately be met from the resources within the city itself. Infact counter insurgency forces are more heavily concentrated, more vulnerable and less able to retaliate in areas of population density than in the countryside. The arms, Kot, supplies and store of the SFs would be more vulnerable to attack by the insurgent in a city. Though it equally applies to guerrillas who also would find it difficult to conceal their stores and supply etc from the CI force who will be looking for it.

**Mobility and Surprise**: These are the key elements in insurgent strategy. Certainly, city streets, windows, roof tops offer space for tatical surface, mobility and hides to disappear or mix in the crowd.

**Terrorism and Sabotage**: Terrorism and sabotage are critical insurgent tactics that thrive in the city where targets abound. It is said that the less dense the population, the less numerous the terrorists because there are fever people to deal with and they encounter more difficulties of survival. Sabotage and terrorism are particularly effective in the urban area since insurgencts look for destroying and damaging the existing set up, effect of which are immediately felt by the population and government.

The political aim of guerrilla as emphasized by Mao Tsa Tung is "guerrilla warfare must fail if its political objectives do not coincide with the aspirations of the people and their sympathy, cooperation and assistance can not be gained." Dissident groups may be even more obivious and vocal in the city than in the countryside due to the number of people involved, their concentration and their ability to confront the government directly. While there are exceptions, most major principles and tactics of the insurgents can be applied with as much validity to the city as to the countryside. The insurgents can never arise by themselves in the suburbs, it is always led from outside the city. And if the counter insurgency force is already trained, prepared and properly organised for urban insurgency, it will be that much easier to contain and suppress the insurgency and avoid that much less loss to lives and property.

The urban insurgents face a number of disadvantages compared with its counterpart. Conventional war with the guerrillas is very difficult in the city without base areas and active rural supports. Though their acitvities in urban areas can be distructive and more harmful and can badly affect the civil administration, which can even be brought to grinding halt.

The insurgent in the cities will be confronted by the C I force that has better communications and greater mobility than in the difficult terrain of rural areas. With the quick intelligence collection the government can employ C I force rapidly to thwart insurgent actions. In combating the insurgent in the city the C I force will find that certain problems become significant, in which they will be restricted in use of certain weapons which would be much superior to the ones insurgent generally have. Even use of excessive force may result in loss of people and property thereby losing popular support of own people. This danger of over reaction is constantly present and the C I force to get rid of a few terrorists plays into the hands of insurgents. Many insurgents moves are calculated to produce just this type of reprisal in the hope that resultant destruction and loss of lives will alienate the friendly population.

The actual combating of an urban insurgency presents a need for both new ideas and refinement of old ones. There isa requirement of training CI force and the police extensively in the techniques peculiar to urban warfare. Upto date and complete knowledge of cities that could present potential problems is also necessary. This should include complete layout plan of the city, population distribution, routes, possible trouble sports etc. More effective weapons are required. The primary problems in insurgency operations, are locating, isolating and eleminating the insurgents. This must, in the end, be the key to success.

It sould be clear that insurgency never arise by itself in sub urban area. It will begin only when a favourable environment has been created by others and the insurgents will always be under the direct control of superior, situated outside. Therefore the operation of the insurgents will not be independent but part of overall strategic plans. They will only do what is told to them, but whatever be the assignment, endeavours would be to do it with perfection. Generally these insurgents work in a group of three to four, since terrain is very unfavourable where risk of exposure are tremendous. The essential quality of an insurgent in sub urban operation are, discipline, probably to a degree unexcelled by any other, and ofcource his descretion. He does not count on more than two to three houses where he can get food, since encirclement inside a house would be fetal. His only armament is his weapon, which will not hamper him while running. For subotage he needs good saws, dynamites and other items, which could even be reached when needed. Even civilian contact may help them in this operation.

The importance of urban insurgency should be fully appreciated and understood. When done effectively and extended over a wide area, it completely paralyses the everyday life of the local population of the area. The population becomes restless, anguished, almost against the development of violence, in order to bring the matter to an end. If at the very start of the insurgency a well organised and trained counter insurgency forces is earmarked, quicker action can be obtained, more lives saved and insurgents are brought down quickly.

## Likely Future Trends in Insurgency

Geography is always a dominating factor in any kind

of warfare. In case of guerrilla warfare or insurgency, because of their being inferior in strength, weapons, and transport etc., terrain plays a predominatly big role which may help them compensate other indequecies in their oranisation. The geographic characteristies of several areas with insurgents potential may involve ie sea, backwaters or any other water channel. Some of these do demonstrate their strategic value for home grown or from outside insurgency. There may be situations in Indian contexts also particularly in our coastal areas and some Southern states where insurgents potential may be hydraulic. In a riverine or onshore enviornment, the insurgent moves in sampans and junks. He interwines his operations with the longstanding patterns of fisherman, rice farmers or transporters. Large segments of population have developed social and economic habits that characterise their culture composition. A few lessons learnt from Sri Lankan operation may be a useful guide.

To defeat an insurgent who for a long time has been part of that composition, the CI force has be organised and trained to effectively intercept insrugents freedom of movement on the water ways, inland and coastal. They must be able to cut off the water ways over which come critical supplies and people from sources friendly to the insurgents.

The insurgent tactic in this environment is generally to insinuate his operations into habitual customs of innocent travel and commerce on the waterways. Before actual interdiction can occur, insurgent need to be detected. In most cases, it is only by overt hostile action that an insurgent reveals his real reason for movement. Main guerrilla or insurgent group can be detected and liquidated if they appear en masse. Their movement of raw material, supplies etc. are all very difficult to detect. The insurgent make use of propaganda against the C I force, since they have been freely using the waterways for centuries. The need to vary rules in accordance with local fishing customs, small farming practices, and early market travel- and at times local smuggling activities, complicate the task of discriminating between hostile and non hostile. The situation also provides a tactical ambush and mining advantage to the insurgent.

There is a need to seriously think and plan for such a contingency so that CI force is not caught unprepared and government napping, running around to find last minute solutions. Planner of waterways CI operations-should in advance plan for such an eventuality by organising and training CI force, ready to meet the strategic requirement of government. Close study of local cultural patterns, transport modes of these waterborne areas, the social habits followed by a valid planning will prove very useful. Follow-on research with the application of lesson learned in similar limited operations in Sri Lanka, will have to be conducted New concepts of waterborne civic action platforms and teams to be exploited.

# 10

# State of Internal Security: As on Date (A Synopsis)

It should be clearly understood that prospects and development of insurgency depends on the attitude of people in the area, where it breeds, their willingness to help the insurgents by providing them intelligence, and supplies and at the same time not cooperating with own security forces who are involved in Counter Insurgency operations. Insurgency operation is the weapon which weaker side uses and as such their tactics would mainly be to hit and run. Any government which consistantly fails in its obligations to cater for the basic needs of the population, will always give way to such a rebellion by their own people. Because of the acquisition of nuclear capabilities by various nations, conventional war has become very rare for the fear of its escalating into nuclear war, which will always be devastaing. Nations therefore resort to guerrilla warfare which pays higher dividents than the cost involved.

Maoist insurgency in an ongoing conflict between Maoists groups also known as Naxalites and the Indian government for the last over 45 years. The conflict in its present form began in 2004 after formation of CPI maoist, a rebel group consisting of PWG and MCC. The hostilities in recent past have escalated and the government has failed to contain it and it has affected nearly 30 million tribals spread in the Red Corridor Zone. The government effforts to use Cobra force and operation Green Hunt have not yielded any worthwhile results. The killing and apprehending of maoist leaders brings temporary peace only and the insurgency which appear fading, revives time and again.

The Naxalite insurgency was characterised by the communists principles on which movement was founded. Fighting for land reforms, the rebels gained support from impoverished population of Eastern and Central India. Thereafter the maoist rebels quickly adopted violence and terror as the core instrument of struggle against the government. Initially they started damaging government infrastructures, looting police station to acquire weapons and damaging railway lines etc. to get recognisation of their potential. Due to poor response of the government to these activities, the insurgents spread beyond West Bengal to neighbouring states and maoist rebels firmly entrenched in remote areas.

The government even today is busy in urban security and urban development. There have been number of projects by the government for rural and tribal development but the nexus between the corrupt officials and the political leaders does not let the benefit reach the masses for who it was meant. The poor still remains in that state and the insurgents take advantage of this state of affair to alieniate the local tribals. Unless the government is serious about the overall development of these tribals including land reforms/ ceiling act and payment of compensation to them, no use of force would help settle this burning issue, which is fast escalating and taking a deadly shape.

Another barrier which restricts finding a workable solution is the personal interest of the local politicians in the area. As internal security is a state subject and they are responsible to deal with it, their political affiliation does not permit full blown and sincere efforts to sort it out. It is also true that some government in some states came to power in part, due to Maoist support. Though they are not openly siding the insurgents, but they are certainly hesitant to crackdown on these naxalites/ insurgents. The population in the Red Corridor will always play an important role in the political landscape of the area. Communist parties have always been the sympathisers of the naxalites.

One of the reasons of high casuality rate on part of the CRPF is the domination of the vast and difficult terrain with inadequate manpower. These troops are employed all over the country and moved at a short notice, this debars them of any experience of the operation in any particular area. They are not specially trained for counter insurgency operations. For the CI operations, they do not have requisite equipment like bullet proof jackets, night vision devices, thermal sensors and equipment to deal with IEDs etc. In addition to lack of specialized training, everyday long range patrolling with poor logistic support in difficult jungle terrain where all moves are on foot, adversely affacts the moral of the force. Use of air power to support ground operation when insugents gather in strength for attack could be considered discreetly. If it violates the norms, at least active use of drones, use of armd helicopter in an emergency to extricate own troops could be considered, in addition to casuality evacution and transportation etc. The NSG is already conducting slithering training from helicopter for the CI force.

The efforts of the government have failed to bring the rebels to the table to find solution. It is because of in sincere and corrupt actions on part of officials and political leaders because of which there has been no improvement in the living conditions of the tribals in remote areas. Hence insurgents easily win over these oppressed masses. In order to achieve results, government has to ensure strict strong and honest governance throughout the red corridor. All state and cental government resources should be integrated to achieve the objective to deal with the maoist revolt. The recent events have sent shock waves throughout the core of Indian security forces and undoubtedly demands urgent reevaluation of state and centre policies.

As reported, the government has decided to focus its counter left wing extremism efforts on six districts of South Bastar and adjoining states, which together account for one third of Maoist insurgency in the country. This will give a push to inter state coordination in security operations and also to roll out development projects in the area. The chief ministers of the affected states of Chhatisgarh, Odisha, Telangana and Maharashtra in a meeting with central government in second week of February 2015, decided to ensure seamless coordination among central forces and state police, undertaking joint operation to block the escape routs of the Maoists, particularly in the worst affected areas of Sukma, Bijapur and Narayanpur districts of Chhatisgarh, Koraput in Odisha, Khummam in Telangana and Garhchiroli in Maharashtra. These areas account for nearly 30 percent of Maoist violence and such coordination will help contain that menace. Also the launching of developments projects in these areas would help and meet the socio-economic needs of the people.

The situation in North East states has also not been

under control. The casualty rate is still much higher in Assam than other terror stricken states communal violence which has been a major concern in the past couple of years has claimed 95 lives in 2014 in one incident only. Some of the India best security resources remain invested in these North East states and state government and the centres sustained efforts both on socio-economic and security front have not yielding very favourable results The deaths in insurgent violence continues unabated. In 2014, Assam accounted for 168 deaths in 246 insurgency incidents. As many as 144 of these deaths were at the hands of NDFB(S) Cadres. The massacre of so many people by Bodo(S) jolted the government and it was then that the government launched an offensive against them and within matter of weeks the outfit was significantly weakened. The focus on NE though emphasized by the government, has been far behind, the required level and intensity

Even in J&K state despite formation of coalition government of BJP and PDP, the situation has not improved According to government sources, there was serious attempt by Pak to infiltrate terrorist in Jammu region in the area of Samba and Kathua in the begining of the year 2015. There were reports that some terrorists had sneaked into these areas of which two were killed when they stormed Rajbagh Police Station in Kathua on 20 March 2015. The other two were killed by the Army on March 21, when they attacked a camp in Samba area, Agencies have recovered a note from slain terrorists indicating the posssibility of group entering India not just to carryout attacks in Samba but to penetrate deep inside to carryout more attacks. The situation therefore is grim in J&K also which government needs to handle with iron hands and immediately.

Insurgency in North East states appeared waning till recent attacks by insurgents in June 15 on an army convoy in Manipur that killed 18 soldiers and injured another 15. Infact Tripura had decided to do away with AFSPA since situation seemed under control. The counter offensive by the army, to carryout raids on the insurgents bases located in Mynamar has proved very effective and has wrest initiative from the insurgents. The tie up, with Mynamar govt. has also worked well. The insurgent camps located in TAGA (Mynamar) where ULFA (I), NSCN (K), KLO and NDFB are currently based and which requires seven days travel time through thick jungles from the Indo-Mynamar border have been raided by the Indian army. The Mynamar army has also positioned itself nearer the Indian border in a bid to choke supply route of the insurgents. The movement of the villagers who support these insurgents is also restricted due to presence of SFs on both sides of the border with Mynamar, particulary after the surgical strike by the Indian army in June, 15.

Sudden spurt in violation results due to remote geolocation, poor governance and lack of infrastructure and development. Though central government gives adequate financial aid to these North East States for their development, but due to corruption nothing worthwhile happens. The recent move by the Indian PM Mr. Narendar Modi to open road and rail link throuh Bangladesh to our North East States will reduce the distance and in turn will boost North East states economy.

The situation in Maoist insurgency prone areas is no better. Early this year (2015), in an audacious offensive the maoists torched 32 heavy vehicles of the civilian on busy GT road near Gaya (Bihar), which were mostly loaded and belonged to all the states of India. The attack was departure from modus-operandi of the maoist who usually target the railways during bandh. The civil administration was taken by surpurise and were ill-prepared to deal with this situation. We should not forget that Naxals will continue to strike against SFs, to remain relevant and expose the state in poor light. Hence to effectively deal with this menace, the SFs have to understand their tactics and their superiority of knoledge of the terrain. They need to be kept under constant pressure. Having suffered several reverses in the past, the SFs are bringing in some changes in their tactics. SFs have decided not to move in large groups, which presents bigger target and move of large body is difficult to conceal. Hence forth the SFs reportedly have decided to make precision strikes in small tactical groups.

It is also reported that CPI (Maoist) is periodically carrying out survey to measure effects of government sponsored development projects since they feel such moves can wean away the local cadre and villagers which can bring major set back, to the maoist armed struggle. The maoist term such government measures as sugar coated bullets, which can retard their movement. The government has launched "Lok Suraj Abhiyan" in all the affected districts which is cetainly affecting the maoist leadership and it is also reported that the insurgents are not getting recruits from these areas.

Until recently the 'Surrender Policy' was advertised through local newspapers and All India Radio which the maoists do not trust being government owned. Hence most insurgents were not aware of the 'Surrender Policy' till such time it was advertised on BBC which the rebels trust and keenly listen to. The affected state government are now planning to announce their Surrender Policies through BBC. Some of the policies on rehabilitation are very lucrative with packages going upto Rs. 40 lakhs. The rebels find such policies favourable and in the year 2014 itself 671 insurgents surrendered.

# Conclusion

The Naxalite insurgency movement in the country has been a great security challenge. This danger has generally gone unnoticed. The insurgency has generally remained confined to Indias poorest and less developed areas Infact these are the poor living conditions which are the main cause to sustain insurgency.

The outline causes of insurgencies are invariably found in frustration of masses, mainly political, socio-economic or religious etc. India was always a fragmented society which the Britishers tried to unite with force. Such amalgam amounted to loss of identity and freedom for many, which erupted as trouble points. To complicate the matter many religious and ethnic groups, who were sectarian and independent, but disadvantaged, found themselves fighting for their religion, ethnicity, language and culture. The naxalites who protected their forest as their home were displaced by the government when mineral deposited worth billions of dollars were discovered in these forested areas around the year 1967. The Adivasis refused such desplacement and relocation and this led to emergence of Maoist Insurgency.

These Aadivasis have been sruviving by farming and by scrapping a living from the forestry. But these means have been threatened and snatched by the government and have been given to corporate houses The maoist war therefore can be termed as a resource war over land and enormous mineral wealth under it, but also a war for the very survival of these aadivasis. The corruption in these area is also rempant which is turning away from electoral politics and going into the hands of maoists. The insurgency is also the result of government's policy which is capital biased and has increased and widened the financial gap between poor and rich particularly in the poor farmers and adivasis communities. At the same time this policy seems to be benefitting the corporate houses. 750 million Indians live in poverty while 5% of top hold 38% of the total assest. Also as per the report adivasis are among the poorest in India where infant mortality rate is 57% and children malnutrition 73% and 42% under the age of five are malnourished.

It was also reported that Salwa Jadum was also responsible for desplacing nearly three lacs Adivasis. The forest department for creating a national park in Bijapur, 60 villages were evicted.

Indias caste system is also one of the reasons of tearing apart social fabric and bringing in a severe divide between the Haves and Have nots (rich and poor). Though the lower strata of the society constitute a big part of the Indian population, but they have remained deprived of the benefits of the economic development of the country. Almost 60% of the population are lacking basic necessities of life. By the very nature of population mix and in addition influx of migrants from the adjoining countries, India has never been a homogenous society. The multiplicity of castes, ethnicities, tribes, religions and ideologies, the warring groups have always been taking advantage of and promoting rivalries and insurgencies.

The government has launched a number of development projects and pumped lot of funds. But this money is being misused by the corrupt officials and political leaders. The successive governments in the past have attempted a piecemeal solution that have brought partial and temporary results. This problem is deeply rooted in social and economic desparities in these tribal areas where the benefit of various welfare project anounced by the government have failed to reach the masses. Since the benefit of these projects has not reached the people, the insurgents are able to exploit the sentiments of the affected lot. Infact at places these insurgents do not want the masses to benefit because of the fear of losing their hold and influence in the areas which are their strong and secured operation bases, they even damage government property and infrastructure to add to the existing miseries of the tribals. They also want to destablize the existing government and to have their own reign of terror to pervail and in the long run establish their own government.

India is committed to resolve the IS problem. Its strong policy to deal with the maoists shows its firm intent, what probably lacks is poor execution at state and lower level. In order to integrate its efforts governments needs to instill strong and effective government throughout the 'Red Corridor'. The ambush in Chhattisgarh, killing 76 CRPF personnel was the worst attack on the SFs since the beginning of the maoist movement. They claim to fight on behalf of the poor people. As the naxalite movement spreads, government faces new complications related to its most destblizing IS challenge.

The Maoist ideology is based on their own interpretation of Marxism and Maoism that seas India as a capitalist state which they feel should be over thrown by the peoples revolution. They do not believe in Indian Constitution which they feel is biased and partial and favours the rich. The nexus between ISI and SIMI and Maoists has also surfaced in a number of encounters, but the government is not willing to accept this fact. The MCC strategy which encompasses following should always be borne in mind in the CI operation planning.

(a) Politicization of matters

(b) Class struggle through local issues

(c) Use of guerrillas to punish the offender.

(d) organise work unions

(e) Precure arms and ammunition when situation demands

(f) create underground organisation and set up

The nascent states of movement showed contrast between urbanised area and rural area particularly underdeveloped naxalite/tribal areas. The insurgents are mainly concentrating on rural and remote areas whereas government focus has been generally on urban development and security. Hence the trend on part of the government has set a rethink in naxalites to evolve a new strategy to infiltrate in urban centres and gradually shift of the confines of rural corridors. The CPI (Maoist) are looking towards cities for recruitment, sympathisers and other logistic support. This new strategy will certainly pose a serious problem for the government. As the business in naxal prone areas is flourishing, the naxals have made good money from corporates, businessmen and land owners etc. As most areas of corporate development are in close proximity of cities, the naxalites are establishing their operation bases from, the naxalites are establishing their operation bases where they can execute their plans of attack and destruction of government infrastructure.

The seven states of North East India also called seven sisters are significantly different from the rest of India. Most of these states have insurgency and are asking for independent statehood, which partly is due to government neglect. These include Assam, Arunachal Pradesh, Meghalaya, Manipur, Mizoram, Nagaland and Tripura.

The North East states are mostly against Indian constitution. Their struggle for self determination arises mainly from an animosity to the outsiders identified as Biharis and Bengalis and their struggle is built around ethnic or tribal identities and they treat the migrant settlers as their enemies. While some ethinic groups and section of society maintain their faith in the revolutionary politics and independent homeland promised by the militiants for many these groups have become objects of fear and hatered. The support to militancy is gradually dwindling.

The positive results of Andhra Pradesh should provide a pathway to exercise effective control. The success of Andhra Pradesh can not only be attributed to actions taken by the SFs alone. This the state has done by increasing their domination of the areas which had vaccume and was a secure base of the maoist insurgents. In addition extensive training of the state police and their effective employment with correct Intelligence gathering proved very useful in curbing this menace of insurgency. Coupled with the massive change in policing and increase in budget of the police force, the force really became effective in dealing and eleminating the influence and presence of maoist insurgents from the efffected areas.

The law and order is a state subject and the actions

required in this regard by the concerned politicians can not be over emphasized. There should be a good coordination between states and centre government machinery. This is particularly important since the insurgents have established inter state bases and sneak into other states when needed or forced by the offensive action by the Security Forces (SFs). The intelligence sharing system should also be geared up and coordinated so that actionable information does not go waste and we lose opportune moment to deal with the insurgents.

The state police also need to be properly trained, motivated, well equipped and well paid so that their willing participation to deal with this menace is always forthcoming. Preferable local youth, who know the terrain, language, people and the cause of insurgency should be recruited. Such youth if trained and motivated properly would always like their state and people to flourish. State police force should also be specially constituted and trained to deal with the naxal problem like the Assam Rifles in the North East states.

In the absence of federal forces, state police are responsible for the security of their state. It is noticed that in areas of naxal insurgency, the state police presence is very sparse. They have at places become target of insurgents attacks, due to their lack of proper training, equipment, motivation and dedicated leadership. States and centre governments have been criticized for their shortage of trained counter insurgency force, in size, equipment, training, structure and also the age profile On the other hand where there have been centralized efforts to coordinate the use of force and economic development, these have largely failed due to poor coordination, corruption and lack of will for the cause, at all levels in the state machinery. The recent events have sent shock waves throughout the ranks and file of the security forces and undoubtedly need a rethink at all levels of governance and execution. A comprehensive strategy need to be developed to ensure bright future of overall country image for the world outside.

The government indeed is committed to address all the problems of the affected people in the insurgency infested areas, like land reforms, appropriate compensation and the focus on development like roads, building, bridges, hospital, schools, and railway lines etc. The government need to be little more serious and result oriented in ensuring success of their various welfare projects. Government also need to integrate national and local efforts to form cohesive Counter insurgency operations against constantly increasing militant threat. The government should ensure effective domination of the Red Corridor the likes done by Andhra Pradesh if they want favourable results.

The government to tackle insurgency should think, seriouly to find solution and strike a balance between security and development. The accepted trend globally is to address development first like education, finances to reduce poverty, health care etc. which are the underlying causes of conflict. At the same time adequate security is also needed to ensure implementation of welfare projects unhindered by the miscreents. It is correctly said that security without development is questronable while the development without security is impossible.

Adequately addressing this problem of insurgency and terrorism will prove essential to project India, image in the rising world power and also exhibit its potential to deal with such Internal Security problems at ease.

**Armed Forces Special Power Act (AFSPA).** This special

Act promulagated after lot of delibrations by the government to provide certain legal safeguards to Army, while operating against militants and terrorists who threaten the sovereignty of India. This is applicable in a few designated disturbed areas only, where necessity to carryout search without warrant and power to arrest and interrogate suspected terrorists/insurgents. The Act grants immunity for the Indian Armed Forces by stipulating that "No presecution, suit to other legal proceedings shall be instituted, except with the previous saction of the central government against any person". The Act provides cover for those who are round the clock involved in fighting the terrorist/insurgents, who are mostly sponsored by the enemy countries. Though the local population in certain disturbed areas do not like this legal cover provided to a soldier, who risks his life for the honour and independence of the country, far away from his own home state in a hostile terrain and environment He has no perosonal interests or enimity with anyone either locals or the terrorists, but is devoted and dedicated to perform duties even at the risk to lose his own life. The allegation of fake encounters, disappearance, torture, rape etc. are always quoted as ground by the sympathisers to do away with the AFSPA. The central government having examined all such allegations have found these mostly baseless and fabricated. In any case the Army Act itself is so strict, just and prompt with the defaulters on all grounds including human rights violation.

# Index

# Index